Clothes Poems

Selected by John Foster

First published in the United States of America in 2008 by
dingles & company
P.O. Box 508
Sea Girt, New Jersey 08750

First Printing

Website: www.dingles.com

E-mail: info@dingles.com

Library of Congress Catalog Card No.: 2007907139

ISBN: 978-1-59646-584-8 (library binding)
        978-1-59646-585-5 (paperback)

© Oxford University Press
This U.S. edition of *Clothes Poems*, originally published in English in 2004, is published by arrangement with Oxford University Press.

Acknowledgments
The editor and publisher wish to thank the following who have kindly given permission for the use of copyright material:

Clare Bevan for "Dressing Up", © Clare Bevan 2004
Paul Cookson for "My Mom's Hat", originally published as "My Mum's Hat", © Paul Cookson 2004
Celia Warren for "Lots of Socks", © Celia Warren 2004

Illustrations by
Jan Lewis; Mary McQuillan; Eric Smith

Printed in China

.·. • dingles &company

My Mom's Hat

My mom has a hat. It is big
  and red.
When I put it on, it goes over
  my head.

It keeps me dry when it is
   snowing.
But I can't see where I am
   going.

Paul Cookson

Lots of Socks

Green socks, blue socks,
yellow socks, red socks,

old socks, new socks,
school socks, bed socks.

Long socks, short socks,
baby socks, sport socks,

odd socks, "posh" socks,
lost-in-the-wash socks.

Celia Warren

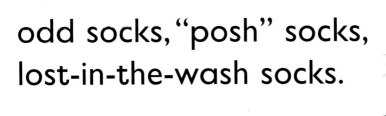

7

Dressing Up

One fox
in yellow socks.

Two kangaroos
in blue shoes.

Three goats
in green coats.

Four brown rats
in big red hats.

And five elephants
in black-and-white pants.

Clare Bevan

Weather Poems

Selected by John Foster

First published in the United States of America in 2008 by
dingles & company
P.O. Box 508
Sea Girt, New Jersey 08750

First Printing

Website: www.dingles.com

E-mail: info@dingles.com

Library of Congress Catalog Card No.: 2007907139

ISBN: 978-1-59646-584-8 (library binding)
      978-1-59646-585-5 (paperback)

Acknowledgments
The editor and publisher wish to thank the following who have kindly given permission for the use of copyright material:

John Foster for "Flying My Kite" and "The Snowball", © John Foster 2004
Roger Stevens for "Rainbow", © Roger Stevens 2004
Erica Stewart for "Wet", © Erica Stewart 2004
Brenda Williams for "We Like", © Brenda Williams 2004

Illustrations by
Rebecca Archer; Tim Benton c/o Linda Rogers Associates;
Paul Gibbs c/o Linda Rogers Associates; John MacGregor; Peter Rutherford

Printed in China

We Like

We like it where there's fog,
and we can't see where to go.

We like it when there's ice.
We like it when there's snow.

Brenda Williams

Flying My Kite

See my kite. Look at it fly.
See my kite up in the sky.

See my kite fly over me.
See my kite up in the tree!

John Foster

The Snowball

Let's make a snowball.
There's lots of snow.

See our snowball
grow and grow!

Pat the snowball.
Pat the snow.

Push the snowball.
Look out!
Oh, no!

John Foster

Rainbow

In the rain
I wear a "mac."
Water drips
down my back.

The sun comes out,
the cloud goes by,
and there's a rainbow
in the sky.

Roger Stevens

23

Wet

Skip. Hop. Skip. Hop.
Skipping in the rain.
Look out! Oh no!
Dripping wet again.

Erica Stewart